FINGERPRINT ANIMALS

by Bobbie Nuytten

PICTURE WINDOW BOOKS
a capstone imprint

Welcome to the fun world of fingerprint art!

Make your own mooing cow or barking dog with your fingers! Did you know that a fingerprint can be the start of a piece of art? Use the following pages to help you make your own animal creations!

Here's what you'll need to get started:

ink

Use an ink pad that's labeled washable. You can pick any size or shape you like. You can even use your favorite color!

pens

Find a pen or marker with a fine tip. An artist pen from a craft store will work too. Use the pen to add shapes and lines to your fingerprints.

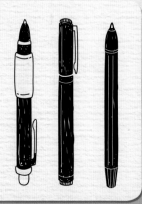

paper

Pick the paper you like best. Smooth computer paper will show the lines in your fingerprints. You can also use thicker paper from a craft store.

FINGERPRINT TIPS

Use different parts of your finger to change the animal's size and shape.

Use the center of your finger or thumb to make oval shapes with lots of lines.

Use the tip of your finger to make small round shapes. Try using the side of your pinky finger for really small shapes.

Use the side of your finger to make long, skinny shapes.

Press down hard on the paper to make your fingerprint darker. A lighter touch will make your fingerprint lighter.

soft sheep

perky pig

clucking chicken

happy cow

4

crawling lizard

spiky hedgehog

jumping kangaroo rat

slow tortoise

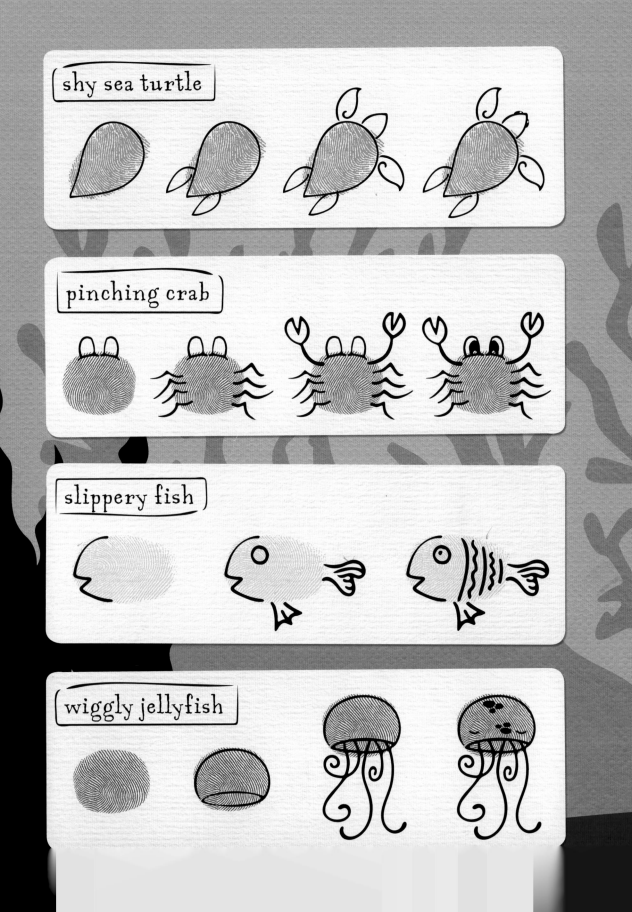

purring cat

barking dog

fluffy bunny

chirping bird

12

sneaky raccoon

sleepy deer

wise owl

14

clever fox

slithering snake

hungry tiger

playful monkey

colorful toucan

hiding turtle

waddling duck

croaking frog

18

furry otter

hopping kangaroo

prickly echidna

cute koala

feathery emu

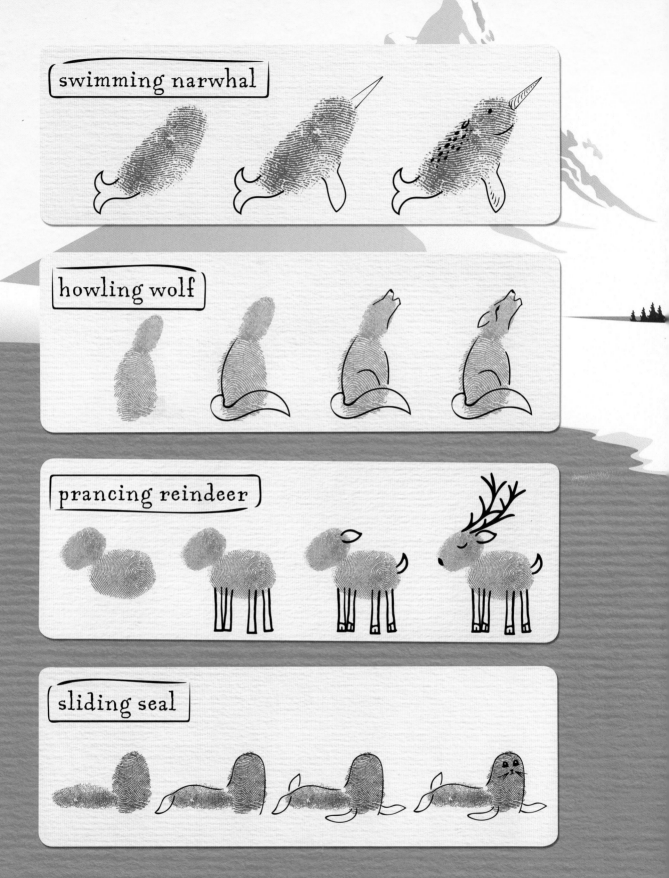

swimming narwhal

howling wolf

prancing reindeer

sliding seal

22

For Lexi and Mia—you taught me to see masterpieces in every scribble.

About the Illustrator

Bobbie Nuytten lives in southern Minnesota with her husband, two young daughters, two golden retrievers, and cat. She has been a designer for over 14 years, focusing on children's books for the last 12 years. Bobbie has always been an avid crafter. In recent years she has been interested in making art and crafts accessible and fun for kids, especially her daughters.

Read More

Bergin, Mark. *It's Fun to Draw Farm Animals.* New York: Sky Pony Press, 2012.

Bolte, Mari. *Drawing Pets: A Step-by-Step Sketchbook.* My First Sketchbook. North Mankato, Minn.: Capstone Press, 2015.

Cuddy, Robbin. *All About Drawing Farm & Forest Animals.* Irvine, Calif.: Walter Foster, 2014.

Internet Sites

FactHound offers a safe, fun way to find Internet sites related to this book. All of the sites on FactHound have been researched by our staff.

Here's all you do:

Visit *www.facthound.com*

Type in this code: 9781479586875

 **Super-cool stuff!** Check out projects, games and lots more at **www.capstonekids.com**

Editor: Michelle Hasselius
Designer: Bobbie Nuytten
Creative Director: Nathan Gassman
Production Specialist: Lori Blackwell

The illustrations in this book were created with pen and ink, and digital collage.

Picture Window Books are published by Capstone,
1710 Roe Crest Drive, North Mankato, Minnesota 56003 www.mycapstone.com

Library of Congress Cataloging-in-Publication Data
Cataloging-in-publication information is on file with the Library of Congress.
ISBN 978-1-4795-8687-5 (library binding)
ISBN 978-1-4795-8691-2 (eBook PDF)

Photographs and background elements from Shutterstock.

Printed in the United States of America in North Mankato, Minnesota.
042016   009710R

Look for all four titles to find more ways to have fun with fingerprints!

FINGERPRINT ANIMALS

FINGERPRINT BUGS

FINGERPRINT CHARACTERS

FINGERPRINT VEHICLES